PRAISE FOR *CHEERLEADERSHIP*

"Stefanie's cheer analogies seamlessly translate into the everyday office and create a space to help you understand your team better, how to motivate them, and how to keep them engaged. With actionable strategies and real-life anecdotes, this is a must-read for anyone aspiring to uplift and lead with enthusiasm!"

—MELISSA BUCCI
Director of Sales and Marketing, Embassy Suites by Hilton Wilmington Riverfront

"It's time to rethink all of our preconceptions about leadership—they're not helping anyone, especially our leaders and leaders-in-the-making. Stefanie Adams cuts through the bluster and shows us how much we can learn from a framework and mindset rooted in the tenets and practices of cheerleading and coaching. Authored with everyone in mind, *CheerLEADERship* raises the bar higher for all of us."

—MARK CROWLEY
Speaker and author of *Lead from the Heart: Transformational Leadership for the 21st Century*

"One of the best ways to succeed as a team or 'squad' is to have a leader that is cheering for you. This beautiful road map to being a 'CheerLEADER' is exactly what you need. Enjoy the read, and benefit from the wisdom."

—CHESTER ELTON
Organizational culture, employee engagement, and leadership expert; bestselling author of *The Carrot Principle* and *Leading with Gratitude*

"*CheerLEADERship* is an easy read packed with sound, practical advice on how to be a motivational leader. Both new and seasoned leaders will glean nuggets of actionable tips on developing their individual team members to build a strong, cohesive, and collaborative team."

—DONNA ESTEVES
(Retired) North America Regional Supply Chain Manager, Corning

"Stefanie is an enthusiastic leader who listens and develops human capital. *CheerLEADERship* was such an inspiration for me as a school superintendent. It brought forth quality day-to-day coaching and leadership development that aligns with 'right-there' leadership."

—DR. CHARLES FOUST
Superintendent, New Hanover County Schools

"*CheerLEADERship* captures the positive change in leadership this world needs right now, given the drastic shifts in workforce and workplace. The model, as described in the book, is interesting, well-designed, and offers many excellent strategies for even the earliest frontline leader to use in their day-to-day work to create high functioning, engaged, results-driven teams."

—LAKEN GREENWOOD
Learning and Organizational Development Specialist, Simpson Strong-Tie

"*CheerLEADERship* is an approachable mindset for millennial leaders who are unlearning antiquated corporate management tactics and tasked with reinventing leadership to work for today's workforce. We're the bridge between many out-of-touch business founders and their future leaders, and *CheerLEADERship* is such a refreshing framework to have in our tool kit."

—KATIE HANNAFIN
Director, Project Management, VaynerMedia

"Stefanie's experience and ability to connect *CheerLEADERship* to our everyday work (and personal) lives creates 'aha' moments. Stefanie breaks down *CheerLEADERship* to an easily digestible format that when practiced daily can help you build a very strong foundation for your team."

—MARIE MACDONALD, SHRM SCP-PHR
Director of Human Resources, health care sector

"Original and insightful, *CheerLEADERship* will give you the framework you need to inspire the most productive and innovative teams."

—MEL ROBBINS
New York Times bestselling author and host of *The Mel Robbins Podcast*

"*CheerLEADERship* is a choice to be wholehearted, optimistic, and relentless in developing the unique potential in others. Stefanie's reflections on her early lived experiences as a cheerleader and coach invite you to do the same. Get ready to be inspired and energized!"

—KATE SIMS
Vice President of Experience and Culture, health care sector

"This uplifting read is perfect for the leader who is looking for an energizing and out-of-the-box way to support and grow their teams. Stefanie provides practical strategies and activities you can use to foster team building, trust, and connection to drive results and have fun while doing so."

—KELLI THOMPSON
Coach, speaker, and author of *Closing the Confidence Gap*

"A changing world needs new rules, and Stefanie Adams is prepared. To stay ahead of the game, she presents us with a playbook that fosters positivity and support, advocating for a team-focused approach that includes everybody. Instead of relying on tired ideas, *CheerLEADERship* takes things to the next level and gives us what we need to succeed now and beyond."

—CY WAKEMAN
Consultant and *New York Times* bestselling author of *Reality-Based Leadership*

CHEERLEADERSHIP

www.amplifypublishinggroup.com

CheerLEADERship: Strategies to Build and Support Human-Centric Workplaces for the Future

©2024 Stefanie Adams. All Rights Reserved. No part of this publication may be reproduced, stored in a retrieval system or transmitted in any form by any means electronic, mechanical, or photocopying, recording or otherwise without the permission of the author.

The views and opinions expressed in this book are solely those of the author. These views and opinions do not necessarily represent those of the publisher or staff. The publisher and the author assume no responsibility for errors, inaccuracies, omissions, or any other inconsistencies herein. All such instances are unintentional and the author's own.

For more information, please contact:
Amplify Publishing, an imprint of Amplify Publishing Group
620 Herndon Parkway, Suite 220
Herndon, VA 20170
info@amplifypublishing.com

Library of Congress Control Number: 2024909387

CPSIA Code: PRV0624A

ISBN-13: 979-8-89138-254-1

Printed in the United States

*This book is dedicated to my "squad,"
Mom, Scott, and Brayden.
Thank you for being MY forever cheerleaders, regardless of championship or losing season.*

STEFANIE ADAMS

**Strategies to Build and Support
Human-Centric Workplaces for the Future**

CONTENTS

INTRODUCTION 1

CHAPTER 1: Defining Your Squad 13

CHAPTER 2: Connect 21

CHAPTER 3: Care 45

CHAPTER 4: Challenge 67

CHAPTER 5: Celebrate 85

CHAPTER 6: Inspire 103

CHAPTER 7: Go, Fight, Win! 117

AFTERWORD 119
APPENDIX 123
ABOUT THE AUTHOR 129

INTRODUCTION

"You are SUCH a cheerleader!"

Over more than thirty years, that statement has been directed at me more times than I can count. And you know what? It's totally true. Even in my mid-forties, I am completely and unapologetically a cheerleader to my core, and I take no offense to others thinking of me as one. I've built a successful career in education and human resources, and I've been elected to public office (top vote-getter!). My "cheerleader energy" creates positive benefits for those I have mentored, led, and worked alongside, both personally and professionally.

But you picked up a book about leadership, so let's pause on cheerleading for just a minute, and introduce the "why" behind what you are about to read.

If you are a leader of a team of two or two hundred, you know today's post-pandemic work environment has gotten incredibly challenging to navigate. Today's workforce wants different things than the workforce of twenty years ago wanted. In my varied professional roles, I have experienced that shift in workforce dynamics, and I found that if I wanted to attract and retain the best and brightest, it was imperative that I recognize and address the needs of the people that I led. And—voila!—out of this need, CheerLEADERship was born.

Work needs to be better, and to make work better, it starts with leaders; leadership must change in a way that supports the employees of today and for the future.

The first time a member of my team told me I was the best leader they'd ever had, I shook my head and blushed; surely they were blowing smoke and looking to get something out of me. Why else would they think I was one of the best leaders of their professional life? This person in particular had almost thirty years of experience in the pharmaceutical industry, and I knew they had experienced fantastic leadership and development throughout their career. To be included in their list of top three leaders as a thirty-something, I felt extremely humbled.

Over the next few years, through trial and error, training, and career changes, my confidence grew in my abilities and, in particular, my leadership. I recognized the importance of self-reflection to being a great leader, and I started to peel back the layers of management to understand why my teams were happy, productive, and achieving greater success than other teams in organizations I had worked at.

The answer? I introduced cheerleading into the workplace.

According to Google Dictionary, a cheerleader is defined as "a person who encourages and openly supports the success of a person or cause." Such a simple concept, and it's exactly what I was doing—being a cheerleader for my teams. By supporting others, providing them with the resources they need to succeed, believing in them, and valuing their contributions, I was able to create groups of people motivated to collaborate, build, and support the mission of each organization I worked at.

Now, I'm experienced enough to know that when someone tells you that they're a cheerleader, that statement often elicits a variety of eye rolls in the room (don't deny it; I've seen it). It can be easy to be cynical and ignore the power of positive reinforcement, but we need only look at the hard-charging sports world, where it is hard to deny the positive uplift cheerleaders have at sporting events. So instead of balking at the eye rolls, I translated those powerful cheerleading ideas and strategies into the workplace, and that is why I am writing this book. I want to encourage other leaders to do the same, and I will share strategies to help them start if "cheerleader" is not a leadership style that comes naturally to them.

Another factor I found myself having to address when I considered why I wanted to write this book is the critical juncture that the labor force is at in the world of work today.

According to Gallup's "State of the Global Workplace: 2023 Report," more than half of America's working population is actively searching or watching for new job opportunities. Additionally, the US Bureau of Labor Statistics Job Openings and Labor Turnover Survey (JOLTS) reports that there were 46.6 million resignations in 2022.

    These are massive numbers, and they mean something. We are no longer living to work. Employees work to support the life they want, and, if their current employer does not provide the flexibility, care, and development they're looking for, they will go elsewhere. According to data from the Society for Human Resource Management (SHRM), the cost of losing an employee can be up to double that employee's annual salary, depending on their role type and their experience level. In addition to the financial implications, valuable time spent recruiting, onboarding, and time to competency are all drags on every company's bottom line. If we leaders want to retain great employees, we need to focus on how we treat our *people* and understand why the ones who stay with us choose to do so. CheerLEADERship will teach leaders how to connect, care, challenge, celebrate, and inspire today's evolved workforce.

    CheerLEADERs *connect* to build trust because we recognize that high-trust organizations have a positive work culture, recruit and retain high-performing employees, and are more profitable. CheerLEADERs *care* enough about their employees to learn individual motivators and demotivators and to create spaces that allow employees to succeed. We recognize that work-life integration is valuable and necessary. CheerLEADERs *challenge* by going over, under, sideways, and sometimes through the walls preventing our teams from achieving greatness. CheerLEADERs *celebrate* and take the time to say, "Yay you!" for the big and the small stuff. And, most importantly, CheerLEADERs *inspire* the next generation of leaders.

Just to be clear, CheerLEADERship is not toxic positivity. CheerLEADERs don't ignore problems or make excuses; CheerLEADERship is trust, accountability, collaboration, and motivation.

Before we dive into the "what" and the "how," let me provide some more personal context to illustrate where this idea came from.

I remember the first time I put on a cheer uniform. It was a Kelly green, long-sleeved, super itchy polyester sweater with two wide yellow stripes down the front. It probably would have burnt up if you got too close to any flames. That sweater, and its matching skirt, were recycled 1980s relics, and they were both two sizes too big on my lanky frame.

But I didn't care. This was it, the "thing" I had been seeking.

By the time I was twelve, I had tried dance, gymnastics, community theater, soccer, and softball. Unlike cheer, all the clothing for these activities fit. But no leotard, costume, jersey, or striped knee sock pair gave me the feeling of euphoria I felt when I slipped into that heavy polyester outfit that made me look more leprechaun than cheerleader. This was the outfit I was destined to wear.

Thankfully, the uniforms got better over the years; less scratchy, better colors, the correct size, and with enough give to allow for a full range of motion. Cheerleading for me was home. Between the ages of twelve to twenty-six (yes, you read that right, I wrote twenty-six), I yelled, jumped, and flipped for any team that would have me. It felt natural to support others. I believed my team would, and could, win if I yelled louder, tossed a stunt a little bit higher, jumped just one more time, and got the crowd engaged. Basketball, football, soccer, guys, girls, whatever—I cheered for all of them with intensity, and it felt good. Each time I stepped onto a field, court, or into the stands, I found my purpose. But, like all things, everything comes to an end, and cheerleading had an expiration date for me...until I made the choice that the expiration date no longer applied.

After three years on the Philadelphia professional cheerleading circuit, I shifted my focus to the "real" world. I recognized that a career using my degree in elementary education wasn't the path I wanted to go down; however, I did manage to stay relatively close to that path, taking a job at a small high school in West Philadelphia, where I provided students with guidance and access to experiences that exposed and connected them to potential careers. I was able to fulfill my purpose of supporting others and helping them get to their "wins," just in a different capacity—it was incredibly fulfilling.

At school, I encountered a volunteer opportunity to build and coach the inaugural cheerleading squad. I held tryouts and selected eight young women who had no prior cheer experience. As a near-peer, someone who had recently gone through experiences that someone one or two stages behind was now or would soon be facing, my first year was filled with challenges: navigating "girl drama," stress over grades, negative neighborhood influences, and no budget. I had to juggle all of these competing priorities while also trying to teach and build a team that felt confident and prepared to get up in front of a crowd. Overall, we had a successful year, and I discovered a deep love for coaching.

This love for cheering and coaching has never left me. For the past ten years, I have kept a set of pom-poms nearby at all times, at work or at home. They give me instant access to happiness, and I've used them in a wide variety of situations. There's something about shaking a big, fluffy pile of plastic that makes people smile, no matter what is going on in their lives. Boyfriend broke up with you? Shake these pom-poms. The pitch to your boss didn't go exactly how you wanted it to? Shake these pom-poms.

I launched my company, WNY People Development, on February 29, 2020—two weeks before the world shut down due to COVID-19. While it was not exactly an optimal time to start a leadership training and coaching business, the time spent behind a computer screen and my many conversations with leaders, individual contributors, and friends solidified what I already knew: people had emerged from the pandemic unhappy. Not just unhappy with work, but with their lives as well. They began to question what they wanted to do and how they wanted to live. They wanted more: more from themselves, more from family and friends, and more from their employers.

As I mentioned previously, I am writing this book for every leader who recognizes that "work" has to get better, particularly the ways in which we build and develop first-time and frontline leaders. In today's rapidly evolving business landscape, these leaders and the roles they play within your organization are critical. As Baby Boomers retire and Gen Z floods the employee roster (with Gen Alpha right on their heels), your employees' expectations, competencies, and collaboration methods are changing; leadership development must change with it. To evolve these leadership roles, you must equip these leaders with skill sets that will support the next-generation workforce. CheerLEADERship provides simple strategies to help leaders create supportive, positive workspaces that employees want to be part of—and grow within.

As you read, you will discover that cheerleading provides highly applicable professional lessons for leaders in all industries. You'll learn to support "squad" work styles while building trust and improving organizational culture and business impact through the five core themes: connect, care, challenge, celebrate, and inspire. This book lays out simple steps to help you become a more innovative and empathetic leader who effectively creates, supports, and guides collaborative teams, and you'll discover strategies you can apply immediately. I will share my personal learnings, stories, and best practices that I have garnered from twenty years of leadership training and coaching, combined with fifteen years of experience as a cheerleader (elementary to pro) and five years as a coach (high school and college).

Top-down management and command-and-control leadership—these concepts are antiquated, and they don't drive business growth. To get the most out of today's workforce, next-gen leaders must take an individualized and human-centric approach. Leaders must highlight and celebrate uniqueness and diversity because our differences make us innovative problem-solvers.

Today's workforce wants to be valued, seen, and heard. Regardless of your industry or the size of your company, understanding and implementing CheerLEADERship concepts will guarantee improved outcomes and cohesion for your most important asset—your people.

HOW TO USE THIS BOOK

The chapters in this book lay out the CheerLEADERship framework. In "Chapter One: Defining Your Squad," you will learn the descriptions of "squad work styles." This cheerleading analogy describes the types of work styles leaders may find on their teams. In subsequent chapters, you will find a chart that provides guidance and suggestions specific to each squad member and their needs depending on the leadership theme focus.

I would like to share a disclaimer about these descriptions: People are people, and leaders must work to understand the individualized personality traits, motivators, and skill sets of each team member. "Squad work style" descriptions are not meant to stereotype or put people in boxes; they are standard traits leaders may experience on work teams. Alongside each work style, I've provided ideas for addressing each style with a human-centric focus.

Each CheerLEADERship theme has its own chapter. In those chapters, you'll encounter stories and data that support the "why" of connect, care, challenge, celebrate, and inspire. Each chapter will conclude with activities to help you implement "the how." To expand the "how" even further, the appendix at the end of the book includes extension activities and reflective questions to build trust, drive productive dialogue, and increase motivation.

I do not believe that leadership is "one size fits all," so throughout the writing process, I interviewed leaders within my network, representing a wide variety of industries and roles, to hear their opinions and thoughts about what builds great leaders and teams. These leaders shared insights and stories and provided feedback about the CheerLEADERship themes, particularly those that they felt were most important from their leadership perspectives. You'll find the notes from these conversations at the end of each chapter under the "Leader Insights" sections for your consideration as you move through your own leadership journey.

Finally, each core theme chapter ends with "Journal Prompts," reflective questions that encourage you to pause and think about your current leadership processes. How can you develop and grow to support and create a more human-centric work experience for your people?

Now you know what to expect, so grab your pom-poms, and let's **GO, FIGHT, WIN!**

CHAPTER ONE

DEFINING YOUR SQUAD

The first step in the CheerLEADERship framework is recognizing that each member of your team is human. Just like the members of a cheerleading squad, they each bring strengths, weaknesses, and a unique set of life experiences that shape how they work and interact with others.

I get it. Work culture is awash in an abundance of sports analogies, and some of them are just not applicable. But work today is all about teamwork, and cheerleading is the only sport where, quite literally, members could not execute at a high level without each other. In cheerleading, members of the team build on each other to create jaw-dropping visuals.

Many of you reading this book may have no experience with cheerleading beyond seeing cheerleaders at your child's basketball game at halftime, or you may have stumbled upon the national competition on ESPN on a random Saturday afternoon. But to fully understand the terminology and the background of this book, as well as the work organization information that I will share with you, you will need to have a basic understanding of the different positions in cheerleading. As your coach and guide through this framework, I'll be taking you through Cheer 101. Here are some general terms you'll encounter throughout:

◊ **BASE.** A person who is in direct weight-bearing contact with the performance surface while providing support for another person. They hold, lift, or toss others into a stunt.

◊ **CRADLE.** A cradle is a base supporting a top person, bracing their arms under the back and under the legs of the top person.

◊ **EXTENSION.** This is a top person in an upright position supported by bases.

◊ **PYRAMID.** A pyramid consists of two or more connected stunts.

◊ **SPOTTER.** The spotter's primary responsibility is to prevent injuries by protecting the head, neck, back, and shoulder area of a top person during the performance of a stunt, pyramid, or toss.

- ◊ **STUNT.** A stunt is any skill in which a top person is supported above the performance surface by one or more people.

- ◊ **TOSS.** This is an airborne stunt where bases execute a throwing motion initiated from the waist level to increase the height of the top person. The top person becomes free from all contact with bases.

- ◊ **TOP PERSON (AKA, THE FLYER).** The top person is the athlete supported above the performance surface in a stunt, pyramid, or toss.

Another term I'll be using often in this book is "full out." Full out means giving 110 percent to the action being executed; there is no half-assing it.

Although most cheerleading stunts need four participants (two bases, a spotter, and a flyer), for the CheerLEADERship framework, I've added two other important positions: front and tumbler. The front (spotter) helps support the bases with additional strength or velocity, and the tumbler provides entertainment through flips and other aerial skills apart from stunts or pyramids.

Now that you have your intro terms down for cheerleading, I am going to introduce you to CheerLEADERship work styles that you may have present on your team. For the purposes of this book, we'll call them your "squad."

◊ **MAIN: THE VISIONARY.** The main on your squad is innovative and big-picture focused. They influence other members of your team because they lead by example, not words. You count on them to be a steady hand in times of change. However, because they are "big picture" thinkers, they sometimes miss important details. If change occurs, they prefer to be leading it, not supporting change generated by others. Additionally, they can struggle with nailing down a direction and moving toward it. Because they have so many ideas, and take the time to consider the strategy around each of them, they can be slow to start new projects.

◊ **BASE: THE FOUNDATION.** The base on your squad is incredibly detail-oriented. They consider every possibility for each decision; they want to know the who, what, why, where, and how for every choice. They are incredibly collaborative and consistent in their approach to problem-solving. Bases function with a growth mindset as long as they have all the information they feel they need to proceed. That is, they believe a person's intelligence and abilities can grow and improve with practice. Given their need for large amounts of information, they tend to struggle with analysis paralysis and are extremely fearful of failure. This can cause frustration for other team members because bases will not act until they have all the information. Bases prefer to do something right the first time, rather than make a mistake that needs correcting.

◊ **SPOT: THE HEART.** Had a bad day? The spot is ready to listen. This member of your squad is extremely empathetic. They have earned the trust of their team members, and they consider the impact on others before making decisions. They are great listeners and seek out diverse perspectives when generating new ideas or solving problems. Although appreciated for their big hearts, they can be taken advantage of. Because spots want everyone on the team to feel good, they often avoid conflict. They strongly believe in "people over profits," which presents a challenge when they have to decide on making worthwhile decisions for the business that potentially reduce people's roles or resources.

◊ **FRONT: THE PROBLEM-SOLVER.** The front on your squad has never confronted a problem they can't solve because they are learning-focused. When they encounter an issue, they are eager to gather ideas and feedback from others, attend training to deepen their understanding and skill sets, and adapt to changing needs. They are reliable and will typically be one of the first people in the room for every team meeting. That being said, they aren't vocal about their ideas or needs. They seek out others' opinions because they lack confidence in themselves and their abilities. Preferring to follow the crowd, the front can easily be drawn into agreement due to the "echo chamber" effect. They are valuable members of the squad, but they don't necessarily recognize their own worth.

◊ **FLYER: THE DOER.** The flyer is hard to miss. They are likable, gregarious, and most likely the social butterfly on your team. They have a lot to say and will freely share their opinion with everyone (whether or not others are interested). They trust themselves and are very quick to act on a new idea or project. Flyers do not fear failure because they believe they can course correct as they go. They are flexible with change—as long as they are the ones to initiate that change. Because of how quickly they work, they tend to frustrate teammates as they often run over or ignore the needs of others. When things go sideways, they struggle with accountability. Because they like to make excuses and point fingers at other members of the team for issues that arise, others find it difficult to see them as effective leaders, even if they view themselves as such.

◊ **TUMBLER: THE INDEPENDENT.** Your tumbler

knows everything about a particular topic or process. They are your subject matter experts (SMEs), and they take pride in that distinction. They are the experts and may gatekeep to keep it that way. Tumblers are often unwilling to share their knowledge with others or believe other team members don't possess the competencies to work alongside them. They are fiercely independent, confident in their abilities, excel at leading themselves, and prefer to work alone. You can count on them to complete whatever project they take on, but they may not communicate the status or problems they encounter during the project. Tumblers lean more toward a fixed mindset, and change can be difficult because they believe intelligence, talent, and other qualities are innate and unchangeable.

Work teams include all types of personalities and skill sets. As a leader, it is your role to support and build on each individual's confidence and competencies and guide the team to function as a collaborative unit. If those responsibilities sound familiar, they should—that makes you the coach! You are the central point that employees look to, lean on, and seek guidance from for their development.

As you reflect on your leadership qualities and how you can rise to the occasion for today's evolved workforce, I encourage you to think about your own professional career and a leader who coached you and shaped your work trajectory.

You can draw from either a positive or a negative experience. Did you have a work "coach" who believed in you, picked you up when you fell, and provided you with the resources necessary to tackle your next challenge? Or was your experience one of fear, doubt, micromanagement, manipulation, and undermining?

If you are envisioning a positive leader who changed your professional path for the better, hold onto that memory and utilize the ideas and strategies in this book to keep building your own leadership competencies. If your heart is fluttering, and you're feeling yourself sweat because I took you back to a place in your career you've tried to forget, use your experience as the example of what *not* to do and take what you learn in this book to be the coach your team needs now and for the future.

What kind of coach are you going to be for your squad?

CHAPTER TWO

CONNECT

One of the most exciting stunts in cheerleading, the one that people appreciate whether they know about the sport or not, is a basket toss. In a basket toss, members of the team toss a flyer high into the air. The flying member then executes some sort of move; it can be a toe touch, twist, a back tuck, or a combination of these. This high-flying, crowd-pleasing move is incredibly fun to watch, which is why it often punctuates the beginning or end of a routine or cheer. To a spectator, it looks easy, but it's not. Learning how to create amazing moments of flight takes a lot of work—more importantly, it takes a lot of trust.

As a cheerleading coach, I found it interesting how eager everyone was to start throwing difficult stunts during the first or second practice with a new team. Some people wanted to prove their strength, some wanted to guarantee a spot for themselves, some wanted to work with friends, and some straight up just wanted to show up and show out. That being said, I never allowed new teammates to execute a basket toss on day one.

Why?

Because it was my responsibility as their coach to make sure that each of my cheerleaders walked out of every practice free from injury. In cheerleading, that's a pretty tough feat, considering that, according to a 2009 study conducted by the National Center for Catastrophic Sports Injury Research (NCCSIR), collegiate cheerleading accounted for 70.5 percent of all female catastrophic sports injuries and high school cheerleading accounted for 65.2 percent of all high school female sports injuries—data points of which I was acutely aware.

In a basket toss, the moment a cheerleader leaves the hands of their bases, anything can go wrong. They are free flying, sometimes twelve to fifteen feet in the air, doing dangerous movements. The people beneath them need to be prepared to move with the flying cheerleader if the stunt shifts in an unanticipated direction, the movement doesn't work exactly the way it's supposed to, or the velocity with which someone comes down is faster than expected. To execute a successful basket toss, the team members working together must trust each other, feel confident in each other's abilities, know and understand the strengths and weaknesses of those around them. It is a truly collaborative effort to get someone to fly.

Learning how to execute a basket toss is a great analogy for a particular work situation I encounter frequently with clients. Leaders identify and pull together a group of talented employees to execute a high-profile project, presentation, or new product launch. The team members have no experience collaborating, aren't knowledgeable about the skill sets each possesses, and lack an understanding of each other's motivators, yet the leader expects them to seamlessly succeed on the first performance. It is a crash-landing waiting to happen because, although the team members possess the appropriate professional capabilities, they lack the most important team component—connection.

BUILD RELATIONSHIPS BEFORE BUILDING STUNTS

That's why in CheerLEADERship, leaders build relationships and connections before building stunts. Although we don't need employees to physically catch each other, we do need them to collaborate with and lean on their team members. Team members need to know they can count on each other to communicate honestly, hold each other accountable, meet deadlines, and work together on a collective goal or mission.

Trust within work teams isn't just a nice-to-have. Data and research continue to assert the strong business case for team trust. Dr. Paul J. Zak, professor of economics, psychology, and management at Claremont Graduate University and chief immersion officer at Immersion, found in his research published in the 2017 article "The Neuroscience of Trust" in the *Harvard Business Review* that "employees in high-trust organizations are more productive, have more energy at work, collaborate better with their colleagues, and stay with their employer longer than people working at low-trust companies. They also suffer less chronic stress and are happier with their lives, and these factors fuel stronger performance."

So if trust is paramount to business success, why do we invest so little time in developing it on our own teams? How often do we hire someone new, put them through one day of company onboarding, give them a cubicle or VPN for home access, and then flood them with project assignment emails from people they haven't even met? Why not pause to create a welcoming space that helps departmental colleagues get to know each other personally and professionally?

As someone who has worked in the HR space, I know if you don't take that time, your flyer (aka, your new hire) in the basket toss analogy may end up in the hospital.

I know what you're thinking. "I don't have time to spend a week talking about our feelings. I hate making people do stupid icebreakers, and they hate them, too." I get it, but trust is about connections, and connecting doesn't have to be super difficult, time-consuming, or "stupid."

I'll give you an example.

I am a Philadelphia Eagles fan living in coastal North Carolina. If I walk down the street, and I see a stranger wearing my team's jersey, T-shirt, or hat, I'm going to yell "Go Birds!" Ninety percent of the time, that person shouts it right back.

Why?

Because we are connected by a common love of team, a common desire to win a Super Bowl, and our common hatred of all things Dallas Cowboys. We don't know each other, but we do know that we are bonded by our deep devotion to our beloved Eagles. That connection can often lead to additional conversation and new friendships.

Learning how to connect isn't rocket science; it's humanizing the people we work with.

As an exercise, poll your team with a "yes" or "no" response to the following statement, "My job is my identity." What do you think their answers will be?

In my experience across industries, qualitative research has shown me that about 85 percent of the time the answer to that question is "no." That percentage goes up if your workforce is made up of more millennial and Gen Z employees. Most people don't want to define themselves by *what* job they do; they want to define themselves by *who* they are.

The next generation isn't living to work; they work to experience life. They are investing in themselves, their health, and their interests outside of the office, and they have captivating personal stories because of that. However, with a line of never-ending projects, deadlines, status reports, and emails that need responses, our team members often can't carve out the time to learn about the fascinating things that make them, *them*. And if that is the case for them, that is doubly the case for us as leaders. If we manage to find the time to learn about our team members and give them the space to do so themselves, they will often find common interests and motivators in unexpected situations—and as leaders, we should capitalize and build on those discovered connections.

Building connection takes time, and time isn't what you have if you lead a team of three, thirty, or three hundred. But here's the thing, there are simple strategies and activities you can use to ensure your team members learn about each other in a way that will drive comfort, collaboration, and belonging.

Connection starts with onboarding. According to a 2015 research brief by the Brandon Hall Group entitled "The True Cost of a Bad Hire," "organizations with a strong onboarding process improve new hire retention by 82% and productivity by over 70%." From the moment someone accepts your job offer, the pre-onboarding process begins. New candidates typically receive a "congratulations" email from the recruiter or HR representative that includes a start date, what to bring, and where to go. I challenge you to take that process a step further. Send a handwritten note welcoming the new member to the team, and let them know how excited you are to have them join. Include your contact information, and encourage them to reach out with any questions between now and their start date. As a bonus—have all members of your team sign the card.

Another fun and easy way to help your newest team member learn more than just their job responsibilities prior to joining is to send a Complete the Sentence challenge like, "I get super pumped every time we have the opportunity to collaborate with...because..." to your current team and then share the responses via email or LinkedIn with your new employee (see additional prompt suggestions in the appendix). Learning about what makes your company a great place to work in the words of future coworkers is an excellent way to build excitement and anticipation with the new employee and establish potential bonds of connection with your current employees.

Speaking of your team, during the pre-onboarding time, encourage them to send an introductory email or LinkedIn invitation to welcome their incoming coworker and begin the conversation. Simple notes of "Welcome" and "Let's grab lunch during your first week" will create good vibes and assure the newest member of your team that they made the right decision.

Once they have officially started, if you want your team to connect, be intentional about introductions. If you work in a hybrid environment, ask all local team members to be present on a specific day, and schedule time for casual coffee talk at the start or the end of the day. If you have remote teams, and in-person meetups aren't feasible, put out a videoconference link and ask all members of the team to join for a fifteen-minute (cameras on) check-in. Give your new hire the opportunity to put faces and names together. There's nothing more embarrassing than corresponding with someone over email for a length of time and eventually getting into a conference room not knowing who the person is you've been partnered with in an endeavor. It sounds simple, but being able to see each other begins the connection process.

For additional suggestions for onboarding success, check the appendix for ideas to build connection and belonging before your new hire even begins their role.

Every time you add a new person to your team, dynamics are going to shift. Due to conflicts or injuries, as a cheerleading coach, I often had to switch out stunt partners. Sometimes the swaps made the stunt better, sometimes they didn't. One thing I could always count on, though, is that the stunt would be different. When dynamics shifted, it was important to take the time to reset and identify this new group's strengths, weaknesses, and collaborative abilities. The same goes for your work teams. Just because you've created a fantastic onboarding experience doesn't mean it's time to let the group go. After the setup, your focus should move into developing intra-team and leader-individual connections.

When I talk about the importance of connecting, we obviously see people as individuals, but it's important to recognize that *how* each individual connects is not a one-size-fits-all equation. Here are a few things to consider for each member of your squad that will help you build stronger relationships.

SQUAD SUPPORT: CONNECT

CONNECT WORK STYLE	LEADER CONNECT ACTIONS
MAIN	- Provide leadership opportunities and options that support development and growth.
BASE	- Assign challenging interdepartmental projects; provide guidance and support throughout.
SPOT	- Ask a lot of questions and truly listen. - Validate emotions and concerns.
FRONT	- Discuss and offer opportunities to utilize perceived strengths. - Identify and encourage training and learning opportunities that align with growth areas.
FLYER	- Identify motivators and triggers early. - Provide space to share successes publicly.
TUMBLER	- Learn backstory; focus on understanding strengths, motivators, and goals. - Create internal networking opportunities.

ACTIVITIES

Now that you understand how to respond to your different squad types in a connect context, check out the following simple activities that will help create and strengthen team connections.

📣 WALL TO WALL

Wall to wall is one of my favorite activities to do, particularly with large groups that don't often get to work together. Wall to wall builds understanding through commonalities in a fun way and then refocuses the conversation on topics pertinent to the work that team members do and the mission that they are a part of. It's super easy to set up; all you need is a room with four walls.

Begin by choosing categories with two to four options, and direct people to choose which wall they want to go to. For example: "People who prefer vacations at the beach, gather to the right. People who prefer to vacation at the mountains, gather at the left." Other popular categories I've used are iPhone versus Android; spicy food versus bland food; ice cream flavors; introvert or extrovert; early riser or night owl; coffee, tea, or neither. One that always gets a rise in facilitated sessions is using sports teams as categories. I live in North Carolina, and if you know anything about our college sports rivalries, they're intense here. People feel very strongly about the teams they support. There's nothing funnier than offering a group the option to choose the University of North Carolina, Duke University, North Carolina State University, or East Carolina University and watch one person walk to the Duke wall, while everyone else gives them a hard time. If you're feeling brave, I highly recommend going for the sports categories if for nothing else but the laughter and the bonding that these rivalries can create. That being said, as I mentioned earlier, I'm originally from Philadelphia, and I know how strongly people feel about their professional sports teams (I am a die-hard Eagles fan who will get in an argument with anyone if you say something bad about my beloved team), so depending on where you live and the sports teams that your organization supports, you may want to consider the repercussions of that specific wall-to-wall category.

Once participants have gone to their respective corners, instruct them to introduce themselves and their role in the company. Depending on the size of the wall groups, ask individuals to group with people they aren't familiar with into teams of three to four. This is when the real work begins.

Provide a reflective question to each of the smaller wall-to-wall breakout groups to discuss, and give a time constraint for the discussion. I typically give two to three minutes depending on how deep the question is. Remind the groups that everybody should have an opportunity to speak. Some sample questions I recommend to deepen understanding and connection between teams are:

- ◊ How did you end up in this role?
- ◊ Why did you choose to work in this industry?
- ◊ What was your first job, and what did it teach you that you still utilize today?
- ◊ Who inspires you and why?
- ◊ What have you learned about yourself in your current role?
- ◊ What is a mistake you've made within the past six months, and what lesson did it teach you?

Repeat the wall to wall process two to three times. The goal is to mix your team up, and give them an opportunity to discuss new topics. Bring everyone back together at the end and ask if anyone learned something new they found interesting and would like to share.

📣 COMMON GROUND

Common ground is a fantastic activity, particularly when you are onboarding new employees. It is a quick, easy, and enjoyable way for team members to get to know each other, learn about what bonds they share, and discover the unique things that make them different.

Split your team into smaller groups of six to eight people. For the best results, it's better to put people together who don't know each other well outside of their professional capacities.

Have each group assign a recorder and a reporter and

then set a timer for three minutes. Challenge each group to find at least five things they have in common—and to get creative. For example, saying "We all work for XYZ company" is boring and predictable; encourage them to have fun with it!

Whenever I facilitate, I like to share a story that prompts laughter and gets people in the right mindset. Many years ago, I led a group of teachers in this activity. When it came time to report out, the first thing they shared was that they had all been arrested. The second thing they found in common? No one wanted to talk about it. That was *not* what I expected to come from a group of seasoned educators, but man, was it funny when it was shared. It immediately connected everyone in the room.

Encourage your team to ask questions, share stories, and think about what makes them unique. Do you have a tattoo in a place no one can see? Do you prefer the *Real Housewives of Beverly Hills* or *New York*? Do you speak another language? Do you hate to drive at night? Beer, wine, liquor, or mocktail? The possibilities are endless.

As each group reveals their commonalities, build additional connection and shared knowledge by asking others in the room to raise their hand if they also "like to eat spicy food" or "have gotten a speeding ticket." Discovering how we align and learning what we have in common personally makes building professional relationships easier.

🔊 SWITCH IT UP

We are creatures of habit, and once we're comfortable with a person, process, or practice, we tend to repeat it. Think about your conference room. I'll bet team members sit in the same chairs every meeting. If they're sitting in the same chairs, they are talking to the same people.

Switch it up.

At your next in-person team meeting, greet each team member at the door, and tell them that they must find a new seat, just for today. Be prepared for some grumbling, but they'll get over it. Sidenote: If the first time you try this everyone simply moves to a new seat, but still ends up close to the person they always sit beside, another version is to pre-place name tents and direct people to sit there. It's a much more prescribed approach, but it may be necessary with some teams that have strong cliques.

Open the meeting with an easy question to prompt shared positive responses like: "What's one thing you've done this week you're really proud of?" or "What are you looking forward to doing this weekend?" Give a few minutes for those close to each other to pair up and discuss. Next, open the floor for anyone to share partner responses that inspired them.

Those few moments provide an opportunity for team members to learn about someone they may not have had the chance to (or have chosen not to) chat with previously. Create space for understanding. Sometimes moments for connection start simply by sitting in a new seat.

📣 LUNCH AND LEARN

Every member of your team has interests, hobbies, and non-work-related knowledge, but they may not share them in the office because it may not feel appropriate. In reality, when we are allowed to talk about the "other stuff" that gets us feeling jazzed up and inspired, it brings out a different side of our personality. Why not allow that "other stuff" to shine at work as well?

During one-on-one meetings, or through an email survey, find out what your team members are into *outside* of the office. Living on the coast, many of my cheerleaders and work teams included surfers, kayakers, and people who loved to fish. I've also worked with others who were obsessed with knitting, Fortnite, community service, and cooking. Once you find out what your folks are into, ask them if they would be interested in sharing their "thing" with the team, including the story of how they got into it, what it taught them, and how others could get involved if they're interested.

If someone answers "yes," set up a lunch and learn. Create an invite that includes highlights about the presenter (the member of your team who loves mountain biking, ceramics, etc.), the topic they are going to share, the date, the time, the location, and the lunch selection. Allow interested parties to sign up, and you're ready to go.

Not only does sharing this information allow individual team members to shine (when we talk about what we love, our true personalities come through), but it also provides a professional development opportunity for the individual presenting to build public speaking skills and leadership. The activity also helps other members of the team better understand what motivates and excites this person outside of work, deepening understanding and connection. And who knows? The presentation may even inspire someone else to take up a new hobby!

LEADER INSIGHTS

NAME:

Kaitlin Choate

ROLE:

Human resources, talent acquisition

INDUSTRY:

Fintech

MOST IMPORTANT CHEERLEADERSHIP THEME:

"Connect. It starts with that first step; everything else will fall into place. Speaking from my personal experience, you (Stefanie) connected with me to understand that I like a challenge."

VALUABLE LEADERSHIP QUALITIES:

"Effective communication is so important; leaders should be constantly communicating feedback. If not done correctly, there's a 'domino effect' of confusion, frustration, and uncertainty. Leaders need to provide feedback—honest, constructive feedback—and then guidance. Adaptability and leading by example are huge; leaders need to roll with the punches or challenge as necessary. Sympathy and emotional intelligence matter, too. We're all human, and we need to connect as a human. Leaders need to tap into their team's feelings, find out what fuels their fire. Learn about your people—that shapes everything that comes afterwards."

ADDITIONAL INSIGHTS:

"The upcoming generation of leaders will be most influential. Technology, [the] pandemic, civil rights, and access to information are influencing them to think differently. They are leading with emotional intelligence, not numbers."

LEADER INSIGHTS

NAME:
Sarah Riska

ROLE:
COO

INDUSTRY:
Boutique salon and spa distribution

MOST IMPORTANT CHEERLEADERSHIP THEME:

"Connect. The connection has to be there in order to build and grow. What does work-life integration look like? Are we honoring our employees' families and commitments? Leaders need to have the ability to see and support what someone is working on, personally and professionally. It's not about you; it's about them. We're all able to understand how to better relate to each other when we recognize everyone is working past their job. Success is found in the growth of others; putting others first is an important component of connection."

VALUABLE LEADERSHIP QUALITIES:

"Leaders must be comfortable and competent coaching others, but they also need to be coachable, always willing to receive feedback and not take it personally. They need to be willing to evolve; if you think you've figured it all out, you're wrong. Be inquisitive. There's a difference between not having self-confidence and being vulnerable."

ADDITIONAL INSIGHTS:

"Generational differences seem so much more vast than when I first began working. Leaders need to think about how [we] relate, how [we] lead; we're seeing more challenges around mental health, and organizations need to figure out how to address [them] properly while also maintaining a focus on growth for the business; it's a delicate balance."

Additionally, help people hone their leadership skills, but be patient because it doesn't happen all at once. Give to your people, and help them become the best version of themselves."

JOURNAL PROMPTS

Think of a time when you felt valued, seen, and motivated at work. What role did connection play?

_____
_____
_____
_____
_____
_____
_____
_____

In your current position, how long did it take for you to truly trust your team? What barriers prevented you from doing so sooner?

_____
_____
_____
_____
_____
_____
_____
_____

What activities have you led that supported trust-building and connection on your team? What would you like to try?

___

What actionable steps will you commit to take within the next thirty days to connect with members of your team?

___

CHAPTER THREE
CARE

It baffles me that one of the chapters in this book needed to be "care." It seems like a no-brainer that leaders should care about their employees. Unfortunately, that's very often not the case, or, if leaders do care, their actions lead others to believe that they don't.

As a community college cheerleading coach, my kids faced the typical situations that you expect most almost-twenty-somethings out on their own for the first time to face. As their coach, I believed it was important for them to recognize that I was there to support them, not just during practice, but outside of practice as well. For instance, when I knew one of my girls was going through a painful breakup with her boyfriend, I would send a simple text to check in as a reminder that no matter how much it felt as if the world was falling apart at that moment, someone was thinking about her and cared about her feelings and broken heart. Or, when one of my girls shared with me that she really wanted to transfer to a stretch school to finish her degree, I made sure I put time aside to work with her on the application essay. When leaders demonstrate what matters to their team matters to them, relationships form that lead to better outputs for all involved.

One of my most memorable situations that fell out of the scope of my coaching duties was when I attended court with one of my cheerleaders—she had gotten an underage drinking citation. Her parents lived four hours away and couldn't attend the early morning summons. I met her at the courthouse, told her everything would be okay, and navigated the hearing alongside her. We didn't talk much, and it was obvious she was scared, disappointed in herself, and nervous about the outcome and potential fallout from the citation. However, she knew she had someone in her corner that would be there, without judgment and regardless of the final verdict. Just being there made all the difference.

This is where leaders often miss the mark. If you do not have the type of relationship where your employees feel safe to share the successes, the challenges, and sometimes the really big mistakes in their lives with you, you can't create a culture conducive to employee growth. What our employees do outside of the office may not matter to the P&L, but those life experiences, interactions, and sometimes traumatic events shape the lives of those we work with. Team members need the space and time to share those stories, which can help you unpack why outside circumstances are benefiting or becoming a drag on their work.

Caring is a two-way street. The same space for caring goes for you as a leader.

Because you are not a robot, you never fully leave the things that happen to you or your family, good and bad, at home. Your teams can read your emotions no matter how stoic you think you may be or how strongly you believe you keep your work and personal lives separate. Our bodies, facial expressions, and tone reflect what is going on in our lives, and you can use those moments to demonstrate to your team that you care about their lives "outside of practice" by showing your own vulnerability.

Here is my personal example.

My father passed away unexpectedly in 2014. He had developed an embolism that ultimately led to his passing a month later. Even though many years have gone by, my body remembers the pain, grief, and emotions of that time. No matter how hard I try, I am well aware I can't hide those fingerprints of grief from the world. Every year in mid-October, I remind my team I won't be myself for the next four weeks, and I share the high-level story about what happened to my dad and the time line of his death. I want them to know that this shift in demeanor is not because of anything they have done. I communicate that regardless of how heavy my heart may feel during this time, I am still here to support and guide them—and that I will get back to my "normal" self soon.

Those few moments shared in a weekly meeting have been monumental in relationship-building with my team.

They no longer see me as just the "boss." Now I'm the boss who has a family and feels sadness just like they do from a time when they've lost someone, an experience that many of us can relate to. That common life experience bonds us through mutual caring, and more importantly, it gives my team members permission to share their stories and emotions with me and to be vulnerable.

The next-generation workforce is keenly in tune with their mental health, and they want to know you are as well.

SET THE TONE—A SMILE CHANGES EVERYTHING

In 1967, UCLA Professor Emeritus Albert Mehrabian published "Decoding of Inconsistent Communications" in the *Journal of Personality and Social Psychology*. Dr. Mehrabian's research concluded that only 7 percent of feelings and attitudes are communicated through words; 38 percent are communicated through tone; and the overwhelming majority of how we convey our feelings to others, 55 percent, comes from our facial expressions and body language.

When training leaders, I always highlight this study because, although it was published many years ago, it continues to hold true (with some exceptions due to the addition of today's remote and hybrid working landscapes).

Think of the last time you went to an athletic event that had cheerleaders engaging the crowd in a chant. They may have been holding signs that said, "We're #1!" But what if they looked bored, sullen, or downright annoyed to be there—would you believe them?

Of course not.

To get the crowd pumped up, especially if the home team is losing with forty-five seconds left on the clock, cheerleaders need to be energetic, in your face, with a big smile that demonstrates that WE CAN STILL WIN THIS!

The same goes for leaders of work teams.

Our face and body language communicate messages to our teams. If you walk into a weekly team meeting with your shoulders hunched, eyes lowered, and a scowl on your face, you immediately set a negative tone for the time you have together with your team. Without words, your team will interpret your body language, anticipate bad news, or feel fear and frustration. They may even shut down completely. CheerLEADERs care about the vibe they create, even when bad news is coming. To help employees become solutions- and future-focused, leaders must set a positive tone, and that begins with a simple smile—especially when we are presented with challenges. We are more adept at solving problems when we have a growth mindset.

I often tell people I believe the reason everyone in our country seems to be so mad at each other is because we spent two years wearing masks during the pandemic, unable to see the smiles underneath them. The experience of physical and emotional distancing hardened us because we lost the ability to read emotions. Intuitively, it would seem that we would move away from negativity. But studies, like "Negativity Drives Online News Consumption" published by *Nature Human Behaviour* in March of 2023, show that negativity does drive certain things. Our brains tend to favor and bend toward negativity, and we make assumptions based on that. Without seeing warm and welcoming features during our time of isolation, it became easier to distance ourselves from those we didn't know.

I am on a mission to combat that. This isn't work-related, but it is important. I challenge you to smile at strangers walking down the street, on the subway, or in a store. We naturally mirror emotions, so if you demonstrate kindness through a smile, nine times out of ten, you'll receive the same in return. A smile truly can change the world, and it's free.

EMBRACE AND ENCOURAGE WELLNESS

I still find myself defending cheerleading as a sport in different circles; how anyone could consider it otherwise blows my mind. To achieve multiple gravity-defying stunts over the course of a three-minute routine with strength and energy, cheerleaders are required to take care of their bodies. As a coach, I asked my teams to condition their bodies multiple times a week: cardio and strength training provided the foundation for cheer excellence.

The physical component is obvious, but what's not so obvious is the importance of an athlete's mental health and mindset. If a cheerleader shows up for practice doubting their abilities, or a situation outside of practice is distracting their focus, injuries can happen. The same goes for today's workforce.

We can't be at our best when our bodies and minds are tired, stressed, or struggling. One blessing of the pandemic is that it forced many of us to recognize we needed to slow down. Personally, I am incredibly grateful for the time I was given to reflect. I reevaluated my goals, my professional and personal journey, and what I truly wanted out of life—and I'm not the only one.

As I highlighted earlier, according to a 2021 US Bureau of Labor Statistics JOLTS report, more than 47 million people left jobs in the United States, with 22 million leaving in 2022. What is driving the exodus? While experts continue to debate this phenomenon, I've seen that, based on my research and conversations with clients, colleagues, and friends, people want more. Earning a paycheck is necessary, of course, but people want to feel invested in and care about the work they're doing, be part of something bigger, and be cared about in the process.

There has been a major mind shift about work post-pandemic—the workforce is prioritizing personal needs, values, and health over money and status. This is particularly true of Gen Z. Finding a balance between work and life is no longer a "nice-to-have" for these employees; it is a requirement if you hope to recruit and retain great people. Over the past five years, a copious amount of research has come out regarding physical and mental health, and their impact on our ability to work.

In addition to supporting mental health, another important part of caring for employees is providing honest and accurate feedback that will drive growth. Too often, especially with young leaders, I've heard the following comment: "I don't want to hurt their feelings." When leaders avoid providing feedback to a member of their team, it doesn't protect their feelings, it is doing them a disservice by not giving them a chance to grow.

Feedback can be both positive and negative, and I encourage every leader I work with to create a culture that supports that. We've all had that moment of panic: Our manager peeks around the corner, looks at you, and wiggles their finger, beckoning you to come over because "I have to talk to you." Naturally, we freak out. Why? Because we believe we're about to get in trouble for something. In caring work environments, that finger wag doesn't incite fear.

While it's easy to get focused on what's wrong, why don't we spend more time highlighting and celebrating what's going right?

When we feel fear, we are unable to truly hear the message being given. When we're fearful, our bodies go into fight-or-flight mode. Our brains turn to mush because blood rushes away from it to help us run faster and conquer the saber-toothed tiger that might be coming out of the bush to our right (obviously, we don't actually have to worry about saber-toothed tigers lurking nowadays, but from an anthropological standpoint, our bodies still react the same way). Leaders can train their teams to understand that the wiggle of a finger doesn't mean something bad is coming. Why not tie that gesture to sharing specific praise for something they did that day? Pay attention to what your actions indicate; make sure that you're not just using them to call out corrective needs but also to highlight successes.

Even if they do provide feedback, leaders may still miss the mark if that feedback is too broad. Of course, I'm going to feel good if someone compliments me and says, "Stefanie, you're great! We're so lucky to have you on this team." But what actually motivates me to continue doing good work is when my leader recognizes something specific and brings it to my attention. For example: "Stefanie, I was really impressed with how you handled that frustrated client today. You used calming language and a balanced tone, and you really listened to what their issue was. Because of the strong communication skills you demonstrated today, we were able to retain that customer. Keep up the good work!"

See the difference?

Positive feedback is beneficial, but if you don't identify specific behaviors and actions, team members will not know what to replicate for continued positive performance.

The same goes for constructive feedback. Too often I've had frustrated employees come to me and say: "My leader told me I have a bad attitude. What does that mean, and how am I supposed to fix that?" In fairness to the individual, that type of feedback feels dismissive and disrespectful. A better way to approach it is to speak to the behaviors that you witnessed. For instance, instead of telling someone that they have a bad attitude, talk about the situation. "Stefanie, during today's team meeting, I felt like you weren't engaged. You were looking at your phone the majority of the time, didn't make eye contact with anybody, and didn't share ideas during the brainstorming session. Is there something going on that you'd like to talk about?"

Notice how the conversation shifts when focused on behaviors, not personality?

As an employee receiving such feedback, now I understand what I was doing and how it was perceived by my leader and potentially the rest of the team. Employees can change actions and behaviors, but subjective statements can be confusing and cause frustration.

Providing specific and actionable feedback, both positive and constructive, is a productive way to show your team that you care. Your specific feedback shows that you are engaged with their performance and their continued success, which is the best sign of a caring leader.

SQUAD SUPPORT: CARE

CARE WORK STYLE	LEADER CARE ACTIONS
MAIN	- Discuss motivators, career path, and goals often. - Walk through "big picture" ideas to gain a better understanding of where they are going and why; have a coaching conversation regarding gaps in planning.
BASE	- Review challenges and provide strategies, resources, and support to help them overcome these obstacles.
SPOT	- Help them recognize when they are being taken advantage of. - Teach them how to say "no."
FRONT	- Highlight learning opportunities when they make mistakes. - Normalize failure.
FLYER	- Advocate for them. - Point out when they have "run over" other members of the team, and have an honest conversation about the impact.
TUMBLER	- Especially during times of change, communicate frequently with them to understand and validate concerns, frustrations, and needs.

ACTIVITIES

It's challenging to promote a caring work environment, especially in a society that can be hard-charging and cynical. The following activities show your employees that you care and will provide them with the space they need to care about themselves and the work that they do for the organization.

📣 WALKING MEETING

One of the easiest ways to promote wellness, a critical element in a caring work environment, is to promote movement. In so many jobs, it's incredibly easy to get stuck at one's workstation for hours on end. Leaders can show that they care about wellness and set the example by implementing walking meetings. Of course, if there is a presentation to review or notes you need to take, talking and walking may not be the best approach. There are plenty of other times when a walking meeting can be invaluable.

For instance, if you've hit a solution roadblock after an hour of working on an issue at a conference table, tell everyone to drop their materials and get outside. If it's a virtual meeting, drop a videoconference link into the chat and ask everyone to connect to the new meeting on their phones. As blood begins pumping through the body, it will help the brain energize and refocus on the conversation. During the walking meeting, ask the group, "What have we *not* tried," and see what new responses come to life.

Another great opportunity to utilize walking meetings is for individual one-on-ones. Again, there will be times when you may need to be tethered to a laptop for certain conversations. But if you're discussing potential goals for the future, mapping out career paths, or discussing a personal situation impacting performance, taking ten minutes to walk around the building provides privacy (particularly if you work in an open office environment) and a safe space to be vulnerable.

Another version of walking meetings provides team members with learning opportunities and relationship building for new team members. Send two to three members of your team out on a walk with the new hire. Provide them with a prompt like the following: "One thing I wish I knew when I started working here was..." A ten-minute break that allows coworkers to share knowledge and experiences is a great way for team members to bond and promotes collaborative conversations.

🔊 BURNING ISSUES

Most leadership research supports the idea that having consistent one-on-ones with employees drives a sense of belonging, value, and greater innovation and productivity. Too often, though, leaders morph this time into becoming a project status check-in or a time to share corrective feedback.

I agree that these elements of business and employee

development are important, but, in CheerLEADERship, great leaders focus on people first. Understanding that internal and external factors directly influence an individual's ability to succeed is necessary—sometimes those influences make their way into the one-on-one space, and, given the insight they provide into your employees' overall job performance, I encourage that.

I recommend the first item on every one-on-one agenda be burning issues. The best way to promote a culture of caring and wellness is by letting your employees know you recognize and value what is important to them, and sometimes those issues are not always work-related. Burning issues is reserved time (typically five to ten minutes) when your team members can share whatever is on their minds. It may be that their dog threw up on the carpet that morning, and they were absolutely disgusted cleaning it up. It could be that they are feeling really nervous about an upcoming presentation they are doing for the C-suite, and they need feedback on all the ideas swirling around in their head. It may even be that they are facing family trauma, such as a sick relative or a looming divorce. Whatever is occupying the space in their brain and needs to come out so they can focus on work items, give them the space and permission to do so. If appropriate, provide guidance or a referral to other resources they can contact for support.

Management styles of the past took a "suck it up buttercup" mentality when it came to the line between an employee's work and personal life. But today's workforce expects to openly discuss these personal situations because the lines between work and home have blurred, particularly after COVID-19. Respect that each of your employees is a human being with an entire life outside of the office. By opening the door for them to share their experiences, thoughts, and fears with you, you'll build trust while helping to assure each member of your team that they can find a healthy balance between work and life.

📣 SHAKE THOSE POM-POMS

As I mentioned earlier, I've always kept a set of pom-poms in my office. I share them with people when they are having a tough day, need a distraction, or a reset. Taking fifteen to twenty seconds to shake them always brings out a smile. As a leader, I challenge you to find your own "pom-poms" that you can share with your team.

What do you have at your disposal that would get people up and moving, just enough to get the blood flowing? Maybe a round of catch with a Koosh ball? How about putting on music and creating a TikTok dance together? What about a relay race to write ideas on the whiteboard? Whatever your "pom-pom" is, encourage your team to use it whenever they're feeling frustrated, stuck, or mad at the outcome of a situation. Simple movement will help to change the vibe and get folks rerouted back onto a productive path.

Let's face it—the world needs more pom-poms!

📣 PTO CHALLENGE

Too often, employee paid time off (PTO) goes unused, yet research continues to tell us that taking time away to rest and recharge is needed and necessary for personal well-being and professional productivity. Be the coach that challenges your team to utilize all of their PTO days.

Keep a PTO tracking calendar for each of your employees. When you notice it's been a few months since one of your team members has taken a day off, or you notice someone showing signs of burnout, create a PTO challenge image and email it to said employee. Include a note in your email that recognizes the time and effort the person has recently put in as well as accomplishments they've had. Encourage them to take a day or more off, if their PTO balance allows. Reinforce the message that work will be there when they return, the team has their back and won't drop any balls while they're out, and that it's a good time for them to slow down and focus on themselves.

Sometimes we need a nudge from others to realize we deserve time away; be that person for your team.

LEADER INSIGHTS

NAME:
Arsalan Hafezi

ROLE:
Owner and CEO

INDUSTRY:
Boutique salon and spa distribution

MOST IMPORTANT CHEERLEADERSHIP THEME(S):

"Inspiration, challenge, and care. A lot of people have inspired me to get me [to] where I am, which has made it possible for me to [make] a difference in the lives of others. Challenging helps your team grow, [and] when they grow, the goals of the organization can grow. Life without a challenge would be very boring. Challenges will always exist. And then lastly, if you don't demonstrate that you care about your people, then what are you doing in leadership?"

VALUABLE LEADERSHIP QUALITIES:

"Leaders need to have an extremely open mind, a clear vision to set the mission, and be flexible. A leader does not know everything; you should hire smarter people than yourself. Get out of the way...if you trust someone to do the work, don't micromanage them."

ADDITIONAL THOUGHTS:

"Every leader has made a lot of mistakes; if you don't make mistakes, you can't learn. Misjudging or setting unrealistic goals can be dangerous. You have to balance between too much or too little expectation. Also, leaders should surround themselves with people [who] challenge them, but [who] also support [a] shared vision."

JOURNAL PROMPTS

Reflect on a time when you felt truly cared for at work. How did that impact your performance, growth, and career path?

_____
_____
_____
_____
_____
_____
_____
_____

What prevents you from providing consistent, honest, and sometimes tough feedback?

_____
_____
_____
_____
_____
_____
_____
_____

How comfortable are you discussing mental health with members of your team? What do you need to become better equipped to do so?

_____
_____
_____
_____
_____
_____
_____
_____
_____

What actionable steps will you commit to take within the next thirty days to demonstrate care for members of your team?

_____
_____
_____
_____
_____
_____
_____
_____
_____

CHAPTER FOUR
CHALLENGE

I remember the day Bibi walked into the gym for cheerleading tryouts. She was super petite, a little awkward, and had a shy smile that immediately drew you in. She had never cheered before. However, as a freshman in community college, she was looking to get involved, make connections, and build new relationships.

Throughout the tryout process, it was obvious she lacked cheer technique, but I was impressed at how hard she worked and at how closely she listened to feedback and applied changes immediately. She may not have been a typical cheerleader, but it was clear she was prepared to put in the time and effort required to become part of the squad.

Bibi made the team—barely. In the beginning, she was one of our "extra" girls—the ones who don't have a consistent place in a stunt group. They typically end up holding a sign in front or providing extra spotting in back. But she was tiny, and, if she could learn how to fly, I knew we could utilize her in a variety of ways.

What I loved about Bibi? She never said "No" or "I can't." Instead, she would say, "I'll try."

Throughout the season, Bibi was a machine. While she may have been nervous about trying a new skill, she never showed it. She trusted her teammates who were responsible for her safety and believed they would catch her. She asked questions of more experienced flyers regarding their best practices for executing stunts with ease. When she fell (which happened frequently during the learning process), she got back up, and said, "Let's do it again." She was relentless in her mission to help our team create "wow" moments, and quite frankly she was our inspiration that year.

I learned so much coaching Bibi that season. With supportive words and guidance, she proved time and time again that success is not about having the most confidence in the room, being the best at something, or having credentials to justify your ability. Great leaders take risks, push through fear, learn from failure, and keep trying.

Hewlett-Packard conducted an internal study several years ago, and the data revealed that women within the company would only apply for a job if their experience and credentials matched 100 percent of the job description. Men, on the other hand, were willing to go after the role if they matched 60 percent of the qualifications listed. That study fascinated me and reminded me that we often stand in the way of our own greatness. If we don't have the internal drive and we don't have an advocate who believes in us, sees our capabilities, and encourages us to get out of our comfort zone, we may miss out on opportunities. We are capable of achieving greatness as individuals and collaborative team members, but sometimes we need to be reminded—and challenged—to do so.

When my son was a baby, he started walking at thirteen months. My husband and I loudly cheered him on every time he pushed up onto his feet, swayed like a drunken sailor, and took those first hesitant steps. It didn't matter how many times he fell back on his heinie, we continued to clap, smile, and yell, "Good for you!" and "Look at you go!" We would then place ourselves just a little bit further away across the room, our arms outstretched to encourage him to go again.

Great leaders do the same.

Each employee comes to us with a concrete set of skills—things they've learned in school, life, and former jobs. However, skill sets shouldn't be static. Recent studies have shown that today's workforce wants to grow; they seek development and challenge. It is your role as the leader to help them see what *could* be, even if they don't yet see it in themselves. Many employees struggle with confidence in themselves, their abilities, and their potential. How can you bring out the best in them, particularly when they are unable to recognize it looking in the mirror?

STRETCH TO OVERCOME FEAR AND MOVE INTO GREATNESS

According to Encyclopedia.com, the definition of stretch is "to be made, or be capable of being made, longer or wider without tearing or breaking." Flyers that pull their leg alongside their head in a heel stretch formation did not start out being able to do so. Our bodies are not naturally built to execute a move like that. It takes time, consistent practice, and movement to help the muscles become flexible enough to push into a heel stretch form.

The same goes for our work and leadership abilities. If a team member can't see themselves completing a challenging assignment or working in a new responsibility, our job as leaders is to not only encourage them to stretch but also to give them the support and room they need to stretch so they can build up to those new responsibilities.

But what happens if we don't believe in someone's ability? If that is the case, it can be very difficult to inspire them to believe in themselves.

In my experience, it is human nature to default to "I can't do that." We believe we don't have enough knowledge, strength, or bravery to conquer even small challenges that confront us. As a cheerleading coach and workforce leader, I have always intentionally focused on each person's individual strengths on my teams. Often, when I highlight these strengths with that person, they are surprised or reveal that they have never thought of themselves in that way.

Doubt is our biggest enemy, and it can be so easy to let the little voice inside our head tell us we are incapable of doing something.

CheerLEADERs need to be louder than that voice.

Remind each member of your team that you believe in them, and, not only do you believe in them, you are giving them projects to push them out of their professional comfort zones because you know they are capable. There is one important caveat here, though. You can't simply tell someone they can do something without providing expectations, resources, and support. Take time to discuss their concerns or fears over the assignment, and address each of them. Will that take longer? Absolutely, but in the long run, with each success, your employee will build confidence in themselves and their abilities, which means they are more likely to take risks, accept more opportunities, and eventually hunt for new challenges on their own. Empower your team to be Bibi. If you create a safe space for screwups, questions, and practice, you will help them stretch beyond what they believed they were capable of.

GO FULL OUT

Preparation for a college cheerleading competition is grueling and intense. It's late-night practices, bruises, cardio, and a lot of defeat along the way. To protect each cheerleader's physical and mental health, I don't recommend 110 percent effort at every practice. Some nights we "walked it," and other nights we went "full out."

What's the difference?

"Walking it" means we are doing the routine but not throwing stunts, tumbling, or dancing super hard. During these lighter routines, you physically move around the floor into each position, but the focus is on building spatial awareness and perfecting counts.

"Full out" is exactly how it sounds: You go FULL OUT! As a coach, when I called "full out," my cheerleaders knew it was time to show up and show out. They would take a deep breath, steady their stance, and put on their best "cheer faces" (these are the sometimes cheesy, sometimes weird, overly expressive, and always joyful looks you see during competitive cheer performances). Every stunt should hit (or at least be attempted with vigor); tumbling should be executed; the dance should be electric; voices should be strong; and every single member of the team should be breathing heavily with a rapid heartbeat at the end of the three-minute routine. Full out is not the time to do just enough to get by. You hit, and you hit it HARD!

So do your work teams "walk it" or go "full out" when faced with a new challenge or project?

As the coach, particularly if you want to challenge your teams to become their best selves, sometimes you will have to decide what intensity is appropriate, as well as how and when to push hard.

If your team is drowning because a pivotal member just quit, and everyone has had to pick up additional responsibilities while you are recruiting their replacement, it may be a good time to give a little grace. Help them prioritize high-need projects, provide work flexibility, and check in with each member to offer support in the way their work style prefers.

However, sometimes you're going to have team members want to "walk it" when you know they're capable of more. When we feel bored, undervalued, or are considering a change of profession, we may begin to phone it in. We show up, do what needs to be done (enough to not attract negative attention), and then leave. The work is getting done, but it's not a healthy place to live permanently; not for the individual, the team, or the organization as a whole.

Remember, all employees seek purpose in their professional lives, no matter how disconnected they may seem. If you are noticing a member of your team doing the bare minimum, get in there and figure out why. They may need a reminder of how capable they are when firing on all cylinders, or they may want to be assigned a high-profile project in an area they are interested in learning more about. Whatever it is, have a good conversation to learn what is preventing them from going "full out," and be prepared for a range of answers: burnout, distraction, misalignment with company mission, feelings of detachment from the team.

Regardless of your team member's response, a good coach can help them work through each challenge to get them back to peak performance again.

As a leader and a coach, you can take active steps to help your work squad overcome obstacles and stretch themselves to tackle even the most difficult challenges.

SQUAD SUPPORT: CHALLENGE

CHALLENGE WORK STYLE	LEADER CHALLENGE ACTIONS
MAIN	- Provide opportunities to lead innovative projects and cross-functional teams.
BASE	- Help them identify a growth area; seek out conference or training opportunities.
SPOT	- Assign a mentee; provide coaching and support.
FRONT	- Have them lead a book study or affinity group.
FLYER	- Create a strategic plan that relates to the whole team; assign roles, responsibilities, and anticipated outcomes.
TUMBLER	- Provide C-suite presentation opportunities to demonstrate knowledge.

ACTIVITIES

To coach our team through challenges, we need to create spaces for them to stretch and feel confident in tackling the unknown. These activities can help your team practice for the future and gain the knowledge that they need to move forward through any obstacle.

📣 WHAT COULD GO WRONG?

Fear of the unknown often causes us to stop any forward progress. We'd rather face the devil we know versus the devil we don't, right? But if we identify everything that could possibly go wrong, it becomes less of an ambiguous mystery, and we begin to realize we can problem-solve for most things that come our way. This exercise takes your teams to the worst-case scenario, allowing team members to visualize what could go "wrong," giving shape to the mystery, and removing their fear of the unknown.

Draw three columns on a whiteboard or piece of paper. Title one of the columns, "Action," one "What Could Go Wrong (WCGW)," and the final one "Impact." Have individual team members or teams share action options; talk through the potential worst-case endings; and outline the impact they would have on the individual, team, and organization as a whole if appropriate. Identify which item has the best risk-versus-reward option, and discuss strategic options for problem-solving if the worst-case scenario were to come true. In other words, hope for the best, but prepare for the worst. See the appendix for a worksheet setup for this activity.

📣 "MAKE IT BETTER" BRAINSTORM

This activity creates a safe space for teams to innovate and "make it better." Identify the problem you are trying to solve, and write it across the top of a piece of chart paper or whiteboard. Assign one person to transcribe and another to be the timekeeper. Next, set a timer for three to five minutes (depending on the complexity of the issue). During that time, encourage individuals to take turns sharing any idea they have for fixing the issue; no ideas are off the table regardless of how expensive, impossible, or ridiculous they may seem. Require everyone to contribute at least one option, asking teammates not to comment negatively on suggestions others make. Everyone should be focused on creating new ideas.

When time is up, have the group collectively discuss all of the options and their feasibility. If there is crossover between ideas, meld them together to create a better one. The conversation should continue until the group has a solid plan everyone can agree to use to attack the problem facing the team.

Another version of this activity that is very effective is to identify a problem in one department and invite employees from a different department or team to brainstorm how they would handle it. For instance, if a software development team is trying to create a more user-friendly product, invite members of the sales or customer service teams to the table, and let them generate ideas to improve the experience. These are teams that interact with customers daily, and they intimately understand what customers ask for and/or expect. The intel that they have that informs them about how to "make it better" will generate a totally different list of ideas from what the software team has brought forward because they are so close to the product, and they speak from a specific focus and perspective that they work within.

Especially for new, less experienced, or introverted members of the team, the "make it better" brainstorm challenges them to use their voice, and it encourages and celebrates creativity.

📣 ROLE SWITCH

Great leaders encourage development and growth, and today's workforce seeks options and an understanding of potential career paths—so why not offer all of that and then some?

Through one-on-one dialogue, learn about each employee's interests and strengths outside of their current role. Ask what other departments they may be curious about. If there is a particular job they have their eye on, provide them with the opportunity to try it out for themselves.

Collaborate with leaders across departments to create a "role switch" shadowing opportunity. In this role switch, individuals partner up and shadow each other for a few days to learn the ins and outs of what their partner does. The switch allows each employee to take on a soft leadership role as they share insights about their job, provide basic training, and answer questions relevant to the work.

This glimpse into a new job will invigorate members of your team and help them see that, although their resume says they are good at a few things, they could potentially utilize and broaden their talents in other ways. This activity is a great confidence booster and will increase a feeling of belonging and team collaboration across departments as well.

LEADER INSIGHTS

NAME:

Grady Griffin

ROLE:

Vice President of Sales

INDUSTRY:

Broadline food sales and distribution

MOST IMPORTANT CHEERLEADERSHIP THEME:

"Challenge. If team members are fearful, scared, and apprehensive, we need to get them comfortable being provided [with] 'fierce feedback.' Telling the truth, although it may make the person uncomfortable, builds success if you're providing it for the right reasons."

VALUABLE LEADERSHIP QUALITIES:

"Leaders should work on their active listening and empathy; they need to ask the right questions to better understand what their teams are experiencing and what support they need. There [are] a lot of natural leaders; they know how to coach and influence, and they challenge those around them. CheerLEADERship can only happen if the culture is real and authentic. The culture of how you treat each other and the way you treat your potential customers is real. You want others to say, 'I want to join that.' The associate matters most; not the stockholder, not the customer. People want to know they'll be cared for and listened to. Leaders need to build trust; [then I can] identify what is impacting my people, [which in turn] is impacting results."

JOURNAL PROMPTS

Identify someone within your professional network who has challenged you in a positive way. What can you learn from their example?

_____
_____
_____
_____
_____
_____
_____
_____

How do you respond to adversity and unexpected problems? Do these responses affect how you challenge and lead others?

_____
_____
_____
_____
_____
_____
_____
_____

What aspects of leadership challenge you? What or who do you need to stretch, grow, and become more confident in these areas?

_____
_____
_____
_____
_____
_____
_____
_____

What actionable steps will you commit to take within the next thirty days to challenge members of your team?

_____
_____
_____
_____
_____
_____
_____
_____

CHAPTER FIVE
CELEBRATE

Ask any athlete who has had an opportunity to run through a paper breakaway banner before a game or down a line of cheerleaders shaking pom-poms on the way to the locker room after a big win; these signs of support intensify a feel-good moment. It is natural to want to be celebrated; it makes us feel that something we did was important. In fact, it was so important that others noticed it and were excited about it.

During my coaching tenure in community college, a young man named Chris showed up for tryouts. He came with zero cheerleading experience, but he had a great attitude, wanted to be part of something, and was willing to learn.

I had never cheered on a team with men, and I hadn't coached them; I felt a bit overwhelmed regarding how best to support his growth and skill-building. So we started at the very beginning, the basics of cheer, and I took the time that we needed to safely educate him.

Every time Chris achieved a new skill, no matter how

small, our entire team clapped, yelled encouraging words, and gave high fives. The first time he did a toe touch and landed it without falling over, the first time he neatly pulled one of the flyers into a shoulder stand, the first time he spotted an extension and came in to catch a high basket, we cheered every time. It was fun to see the support—and his growth.

Over the following few months, he became a major asset on the team. He had mastered basic cheerleading stunts, but he knew that he needed to build muscle to perform more difficult stunts. He began an intense gym regimen, and the team got the benefit of that persistence. Before long, he was cautiously throwing single-man stunts, a two-person skill reserved for high-level college teams. With each new accomplishment, our team celebrated. We were proud of his resilience, curiosity, and focus.

I left that institution at the end of the season, but I kept in touch with many of my cheerleaders from the squad, including Chris. Over the next year, he continued to work on his skills. When the time came to transfer to a four-year institution, he made their division one high-performing cheerleading squad—I was so proud of him!

We met up for lunch one day, and he mentioned how important celebrating the small accomplishments along the way as a first-time cheerleader had made a huge difference for him. Even when he felt he was doing something basic, and everyone else around him was stronger and had more experience, feeling the support of others and being highlighted for the abilities he brought to the table made all the difference in the world and encouraged him to continue making progress and build out his skill set.

Celebration matters. I don't care how old you are, or what role you have in an organization, we all seek validation and crave someone else cheering us on, especially during challenging times.

I recently went to lunch with a group of former co-workers. I had previously led the training team within the HR department, and they had worked in different capacities in customer service and product management. I'm not sure how it came up, but one of them mentioned they would never forget the time I walked across the employee floor with the drink cart. For context, summer was a highly productive time and often stressful. Leadership, including myself, took turns providing random treats for staff as a "thank you" for all of their hard work. So why was that memorable? You see, when I came by with the drink cart, I brought my pom-poms. As my colleagues handed out drinks, I ran through the cubicle space shaking my pom-poms and cheering on employees. Many of them stared at me like I had three heads, but those weary looks quickly turned to smiles and chuckles. Some folks even got up from their chairs and cheered with me. I loved doing it, but I didn't realize the impact that that simple moment had on others. The individual I was having brunch with was referring to an event that had taken place four or five years prior, yet they still thought about it and loved the energy I had been able to bring to the room. I had this moment of thinking: "Wow—I did that. I made people feel seen, valued, and happy just by bringing a positive energy into a high-stress space."

At that same company, I had four direct reports. When I first joined the team, they were required to clock in and out through our human resources information software. I frequently had to input or correct time cards because they often forgot. It was laborious, and frankly frustrating, to have to keep after adults to complete such a simple request. One random week, without fanfare, I placed a Time Keeper Star (an actual yellow star I cut out of construction paper) on the desk of a team member who had clocked in and out consistently for two weeks. When Monday came, the other three members of the team saw the star and immediately wanted to know how *they* could earn a star. And thus began the Time Keeper Star collection challenge. Over the next year, I made many more stars than I did time-card corrections.

Of course, we can get in trouble if we go overboard. Adults like to be rewarded, but celebration doesn't always have to come in the form of a huge bonus or promotion (but yes, those are fabulous, too), especially if there isn't the budget for it.

And it's not just about the big product launch; small wins matter, too. When you land a new customer, create a new process, speak up for the first time in a meeting, highlight the small win and celebrate.

FIND THE RIGHT MUSIC

As I've mentioned, having grown up in the suburbs of Philadelphia, I am a hardcore Eagles fan. There are many songs synonymous with the team and its history, but probably the most recognizable one is "Eye of the Tiger" by Survivor (also known as the theme song from the movie *Rocky III*). In the fourth quarter of a football game, and the final outcome is on the line, "DUN...DUN, dun, DUN...DUN, dun, DUN... dun, dun, DUUUUNNNNN" starts playing over the stadium speakers, and you can feel the energy turn. People get out of their seats, arms go up, voices get louder, and the momentum shifts as we collectively cheer on a play that hopefully puts the nail in the coffin for the other team. (Don't deny it, you're singing it in your head right now, aren't you?)

Would we get the same crowd response if "Landslide" by Fleetwood Mac melodically flowed through the speakers? Probably not, even if it is an amazing song.

CheerLEADERs pick the right "music" for each moment, literally and figuratively.

An example for literally, because we've all been there— the final push on a project. Your team is completely burned out, cranky, and stressed because the project has sapped everyone's energy, efforts, and innovation to make a 5:00 p.m. deadline. How can you help the team get over the finish line? Add music!

For in-person teams, pull out a speaker in the office.

For virtual teams, either send a song link with explicit instructions for when to click it or create a five-minute virtual meeting. Once everyone is together, online or otherwise, play the "get hyped" song you all need to finish strong. Make sure the song has a good beat and a positive message. Play it loud and encourage your people to step away from their computers for two minutes to really feel the music.

As a former elected official who served as chair on a local school board at the height of the COVID-19 pandemic (an experience for a very different book), I pulled from a host of songs to face whatever was thrown at me in a meeting. Depending on the nature of the vote, and how controversial it was in the community, the soundtrack for my drive to the board of education building could include Beyoncé's "Break My Soul," Katy Perry's "Roar," or Wu-Tang Clan's "Protect Ya Neck." Music is powerful and can prepare you to tackle anything—I am speaking from personal experience.

SQUAD SUPPORT: CELEBRATE

We've identified differences in your squad's work styles, so it should come as no surprise that celebrating is not a one-size-fits-all affair; these ideas and explanations are a bit more in-depth, so I felt it necessary to break out from the simple chart model seen in other chapters. As a coach learning about motivators and needs, you should ask *how* each member feels about being celebrated as well as what style of celebration they prefer. As I've stated before, there is no end-all-be-all profile for each person, but, in my experience, I have found the following categorizations to be true about celebrating my squad.

◊ **MAIN.** This work style is a bit of a toss-up. Because they are intrinsically motivated, mains may or may not need or seek celebratory actions. However, that doesn't mean you shouldn't highlight their accomplishments in some way. Ask if they prefer public or private compliments, team or personal gifts, or monetary bonuses or promotion opportunities. Share their stories of success with executives, and copy them on the email so they are aware you are highlighting positive performance and promoting visibility at higher levels.

- ◊ **BASE.** Because this work style gets caught up in analysis paralysis, celebrating solid decision-making when it happens is key. Public, verbal affirmation demonstrates that you recognize them taking the lead. This allows them to find confidence in their abilities and will promote the behavior to continue. Also, highlighting moments where they are hyper detail-focused, especially when it's needed for a project to continue, will demonstrate to other team members that there is value in the base's highly specific approach, broadcasting the benefit it provides for overall team success.

- ◊ **SPOT.** The spot is similar to the main work style when it comes to celebrations. Have a conversation with them about their preferences, and expect that responses will be varied. One way to highlight their value and abilities is to ask them to represent the team or company at events or conferences. This displays that you trust them to serve as an ambassador. As an added benefit, they'll come back and be able to share pertinent information with the team. By having experiences that others on the team have not had, they gain the opportunity to be the expert in the room, driving confidence and building leadership competencies.

- ◊ **FRONT.** Due to a lack of confidence, the front on your team definitely needs to be celebrated. Because they so often question themselves, they are unable to see the contributions they bring to the team. I encourage you to consistently dispense specific praise but do so initially in one-on-one meetings. Tell them that you would like to share the accomplishment with the rest of the team, and ask if they would be comfortable with that. Additionally, a fantastic way to encourage growth is to identify learning opportunities and advocate for the budget to make it happen. These opportunities include classes, conferences, or mentorship opportunities all of which act as a celebration to deepen or develop the skills your front is seeking, helping to motivate and excite them.

◊ **FLYER.** Your flyer loves to be celebrated, so go big or go home with this one. Make the celebration big, flashy, and public! Flyers prefer the spotlight and thrive in it. If you have the opportunity to shout out a win on behalf of your flyer, do so in a team meeting, company newsletter, or email blast to customers. The more they get to see their name attached to success, the more motivated they are to replicate the experience. Furthermore, gifts, money, and certificates are fantastic celebratory motivators for this work style.

◊ **TUMBLER.** In my experience, tumblers are similar to the main work style when it comes to celebration.

Some adore it and want as much public exposure as possible, while others are very private and would prefer to receive a congratulatory email and be done with it. Your job as their coach is to determine how they will feel most respected and valued, which can simply be a conversation. Once you know their preference, it is important for you to demonstrate that you listened by celebrating them in the way they feel most comfortable.

ACTIVITIES

Celebration activities are by their nature filled with excitement. They are a cost-effective way to celebrate teamwork and keep employees engaged.

📣 TEAM PLAYLIST

Ask each member of your team to send you their favorite hype song, the song they play when they get ready for a big night out, the song that picks them up on tough days, or the song that makes them want to sing at the top of their lungs.

Compile the submissions to create a team playlist. Whenever your team is doing something big, like launching a new product, welcoming a new team member, or brainstorming ways to attack a customer challenge, play one of the songs off the list, tell everyone the name of the person who recommended it, and have the team member share the story behind it. Take two minutes to get everyone out of their seats, encourage movement (in my case, dancing), and get pumped for whatever is coming.

Music has the power to change a vibe, especially if the message of the song is inspirational and the beat hits just right. A bonus to this activity is that you get a small window into each person's interests. You may have one team member share a Rage Against the Machine song, another who picks a Taylor Swift tune, and one who gets hyped up by instrumental jazz music. This simple team activity provides a space for each person to bring a bit of their own personality to work, all while learning new things about their coworkers. It's a win-win!

📣 TROPHY

Identify a trophy for your team. If you're in the hospitality industry, maybe it's a large, golden spoon. If you're in the financial sector, it could be a deposit bag full of celebratory notes from coworkers. If you're in education, find a stuffed animal version of your school's mascot, or you could quite literally order a gold trophy. There are a ton of fun options out there, so get creative. Whatever works best for your team, collaboratively determine eligibility requirements that would earn someone the team trophy. Each week or month, identify who is most deserving, and to promote peer celebration, ask the previous winner to pass the torch during a team meeting and explain why the next recipient was chosen for the honor.

Encourage each winner to proudly display their trophy at their workstation or in the background of their Zoom videoconference screen.

📣 DRIVE-BY POST-IT

Sometimes little things make a big difference. If you work in person or in a hybrid setup, dropping a Post-it note on a team member's workstation when they're not around is fun and easy. And surprise compliments are a great way to make people feel good. A simple handwritten note stating, "You killed it leading yesterday's meeting. Keep it up!" or "Thanks for jumping in to cover for (name) when they were out. You're an awesome team player!" will bring a smile to the face of the recipient and remind them that they are valued and an important part of the team.

For remote teams, you can replicate a similar experience by dropping a personal complimentary comment in the chat box when "away" is displayed. It's a nice surprise for them when they return to their desk or reopen the chat window. If you really want to go old school, drop a handwritten note for them in the mail to their home address.

In-person or virtual, make sure the praise is specific and recent. Highlighting small wins as a leader lets your people know that what they do every day matters and contributes to the overall success of the team.

LEADER INSIGHTS

NAME:

Dr. Rebecca Guidice

ROLE:

Professor, management

INDUSTRY:

Higher education

MOST IMPORTANT CHEERLEADERSHIP THEME:

"Connect. You can't show you care until you've connected. And I can't challenge or inspire you if I don't know the person and what makes them tick. Building relationships is key!"

VALUABLE LEADERSHIP QUALITIES:

"Leaders must be honest and have integrity. I left a role due to a lie; that is impactful. Leaders need to be willing to hold their teams accountable but do so with humor; levity is important. Curiosity is key."

ADDITIONAL THOUGHTS:

"Your team wants to know you have their back. You have to strike a balance between hand-holding, not having all the answers, and giving them space to experiment and try. When times are uncertain, they need to know their leader is going to be there to listen and remind them we'll make it through together. Also, as a leader, you too need to try and screw up; each time you do, you build your leadership muscle a little bit more."

JOURNAL PROMPTS

How do you like to be celebrated?

_____
_____
_____
_____
_____
_____
_____
_____

Think of a time you were recognized for something positive at work. How did that moment impact your performance moving forward?

_____
_____
_____
_____
_____
_____
_____
_____

Identify two "wins" you and/or your team achieved over the past two weeks. Did you highlight and celebrate them when they happened? Why or why not?

_____
_____
_____
_____
_____
_____
_____
_____
_____

What actionable steps will you commit to take within the next thirty days to celebrate members of your team?

_____
_____
_____
_____
_____
_____
_____
_____
_____

CHAPTER SIX
INSPIRE

How do you inspire your team? Inspiration starts by *showing* them how it's done.

If I expected my squad to arrive fifteen minutes early to practice, I would arrive thirty minutes early. If we were going to run, I would run beside them. If we were knocking out crunches, I would do an extra ten and watch to see who else joined me. The funny thing about inspiration is that it's more about getting to someone's heart, not their mind. When you work as a team, you want others to succeed, which allows for everyone to focus on a common goal. If we are not inspired, we don't give 100 percent.

Countless studies continue to prove that happy, engaged, and inspired employees are more productive and typically stay longer with their organizations. People want to feel a part of something bigger than themselves.

Day-to-day tasks are part of what we all have to do; they're a reality of work. However, when we feel like we are contributing to the overall mission, something that really matters, that mission is exciting and something that people want to be a part of.

In cheerleading, we spend months perfecting a competition routine. The work is challenging and exhausting, and it can often lead to conflict born of frustration when things don't go the way we want. However, when the team steps out on that competition mat at the end of the season after putting in five to six months of hard work together, everyone realizes that the moment has finally arrived. Sometimes the moment ends up with a championship trophy because everything hits and routines go off flawlessly. Other times, you get out on the mat, and everything falls down around you. I have found that with either outcome, if we've done it as a group, we feel inspired because we know the hard work that went into that final performance, and it was a collective experience.

Who are the leaders that have inspired you, personally and professionally? What did they teach you, and how has their presence in your life shaped how you work and lead today?

Keeping that in mind, I challenge you to ask yourself, how do you want to be remembered? What words will employees use to describe you? Will you be the leader who people look back on and are grateful for the experiences shared, the guidance you gave, the resources you provided, and the example you set? Or, will you be the *other*—the leader who inspires them to do the exact opposite of what you did because of how you made them feel?

ACTIVITIES

As a leader, one of your most important duties will be to inspire your team. The following activities are a great way to have your employees inspire each other and gain inspiration from you and the organization.

📣 MY MISTAKE

Although our teams look to us for guidance and support, leaders aren't perfect, and it can be extremely powerful and inspiring when we acknowledge and lean into the messiness of life and work.

Share a story of a mistake you've made in your career, the bigger the better. Be honest and vulnerable about what went wrong, but more importantly, share what you learned from the failure and how it has changed you. What do you do differently *because* of that mistake? How has work improved *because* you changed your behaviors, habits, or processes?

Remind your team that you don't have all the answers, but you are committed to learning and growing. Assure them you will continue to make mistakes because making mistakes means that you are trying to do better than the "status quo," and encourage them to do the same. Let them know if and when mistakes happen, you'll be there to help clean up, advocate for them, and use the episode as an opportunity to improve.

📣 C-SUITE SIT DOWN

In one of my previous roles, I asked the company president if he would be willing to sit down with new hires a couple of weeks in to share the company's vision, provide updates, and answer questions. Although he had an incredibly busy calendar, we worked together to create a schedule that allotted sixty minutes every quarter to meet and chat with the newest members of our team in a small group setting, and it was probably one of the most powerful things I have ever had the opportunity to be a part of.

During those conversations, I watched body language closely, and these new employees, many in their first real professional roles, were locked in. They listened intently and asked fantastic questions. The best part was that the longer they spent with the president of a multimillion-dollar company, the more they realized he was a human with a story, just like each of them. The questions became more personalized, deeper, and thoughtful. By the end of those sixty minutes, true connections had been made, and no amount of orientation slides could have created that same impression.

If your C-suite is willing to open themselves up to vulnerability and honest dialogue, take advantage of that. We want to feel we are part of something bigger and that our day-to-day tasks contribute to an ultimate goal. Having the opportunity to hear directly from the top decision-makers will help your team members connect the dots and feel more engaged in the company's mission and culture.

Prepare question prompts for the event, such as, "How did you get started in this industry?" or "What is an important lesson you've learned as CEO?" to get the conversation started. It's also a great idea to ask fun questions, like, "At a wedding, what song gets you out on the dance floor, and what's your move?" Be prepared to redirect the discussion if there is a lull, but for the most part, let your team drive the dialogue and subject matter because it is in those moments of unplanned and unstructured conversation where you find gold.

📣 "WE DAYS"

Bring your team together for a We Day. What is a We Day? This is a day to review the mission and vision of the company, provide any updated direction or information coming from the executive leadership team, and check in on short- and long-term planning. This is a time when you can have an open discussion about how this work team can support the overall organization, the department, and each other by creating "We will…" statements. Once the list is complete, bring energy to the commitments by saying each statement out loud in unison (like a cheer). Print out the statements and hang a copy in each office or use a screenshot of the compiled statements as background wallpaper on each computer.

Take the inspiration a step further by creating a hashtag

that summarizes what "we" are going to accomplish together. For instance, if your company is in a high-growth period, #nextlevel could be your team's focus. If you are in the beta phase of a new product rollout, #cantstopwontstop reminds your team that you're in it together, and you're going to keep pushing until the product is rolled out.

If your budget allows, order wearable swag with your team's hashtag. There's something powerful about standing alongside your teammates in a matching "uniform" that bonds you together in a shared mission. Throw that hashtag on a T-shirt or sweatshirt, and schedule We Days when you physically demonstrate your collaborative vibe to the company, and more importantly, to each other. Snap pictures and encourage team members to share on social media to show team unity.

LEADER INSIGHTS

NAME:

Ian Harper

ROLE:

Human resources, talent development

INDUSTRY:

Technology

MOST IMPORTANT CHEERLEADERSHIP THEME

"Inspire. For people to do their best work, they have to care about it. Inspiration makes me care about what I'm doing. It's knowing that what I'm doing has impact, and I'm not just punching a clock. You can't do the other things without inspiration."

VALUABLE LEADERSHIP QUALITIES:

"Leaders have to have empathy so they can connect deeper with direct reports. They need to show that they 'give a crap.' They also need to recognize that outside experiences impact work, and they need to adapt based on that. Also, leaders need to get out of the way and empower their people; remove blockers, and trust them to do their job. Lastly, leaders need to have enthusiasm. It's infectious, and it rubs off on a team."

ADDITIONAL THOUGHTS:

"Leaders have to have one foot in the future and one foot in the now. When change is occurring, they need to confidently look at their team, admit it hurts, but it won't always hurt. Effectively communicate, and remind your people that there is an exit to the tunnel; strategically plan and communicate. The leader is there to help them get to the other side."

LEADER INSIGHTS

NAME:

Heidi Karamis

ROLE:

District Sales Manager

INDUSTRY:

Pharmaceuticals

MOST IMPORTANT CHEERLEADERSHIP THEME:

"Inspire. That's what coaching and leadership is. All CheerLEADERship themes are important, but when you inspire someone, you're reaching something in their soul. If you lead, but your team doesn't buy into what you're selling, they're going to do their own thing. It's about being a manager versus a leader;

if you're micromanaging, you are not inspiring. It creates self-motivation."

VALUABLE LEADERSHIP QUALITIES:

"Trust and respect are big components. Everyone isn't going to succeed the same way. Leaders must look at each employee's strengths. People work harder for people they like. Focus and prioritization are also important; everyone has different goals and objectives, and it's the leader's job to manage the noise coming out of other departments. Additionally, if you can't effectively communicate, it leads to misunderstanding expectations, and people may not feel valued. People create stories if you don't communicate. No fluff—communication can't be subjective. It needs to be factual and objective with examples."

ADDITIONAL THOUGHTS:

"Leadership is important even if you don't have direct reports. Everybody succeeds together as a team...it needs to be more than just 'I succeed.'"

JOURNAL PROMPTS

What has had the greatest impact on your professional path? Why?

_____
_____
_____
_____
_____
_____
_____

If you have had an inspirational leader, what traits did they possess that you would like to emulate? If not, what approaches have you learned in *CheerLEADERship* to be that leader?

_____
_____
_____
_____
_____
_____
_____

How would you like to be remembered? What words do you hope people use to describe you as a leader?

_____
_____
_____
_____
_____
_____
_____
_____

What actionable steps will you commit to take within the next thirty days to create inspirational moments for members of your team?

_____
_____
_____
_____
_____
_____
_____
_____

CHAPTER SEVEN
GO, FIGHT, WIN!

As you've read through the CheerLEADERship framework and come to the end of this book, I hope you feel inspired, invigorated, and pumped to lead into the future of work. Remember, every team is only as good as its weakest player, and it's the job of the coach to drive that message home. It is your responsibility to identify weaknesses and figure out ways to fix them, develop them, or bypass them completely by guiding employees in a new direction if needed. It's also your job to amplify the good: scream out those successes from the rooftop when members of your team may not be comfortable doing so. Identify strengths, and utilize them to create those "wow" moments that inspire teams to continually strive for success.

You have learned CheerLEADERship concepts and how they apply to specific work styles, and you are ready and prepared to connect, care, challenge, celebrate, and inspire. It is inevitable that, at some point, you will get frustrated or feel stalled in your progress. When you get stuck on the coaching journey, grab your pom-poms, and remember the following...Go, Fight, Win!

GO! (G=GOAL). Remind your team about the *goal* you are working toward. Identify team member differences and strengths, and capitalize on each so that the team can push through with a unified focus.

FIGHT! (F=FACTS AND FEELINGS). When challenges arise, consider *facts and feelings*. How does this situation impact your team personally and professionally? Address the root cause of an issue, and always consider the human component.

WIN! (W=TEAMWORK). Finally, and most importantly, you've got to put in the team*work* with energy, enthusiasm, and focus. Success doesn't come easy, but with a committed group of people working together, anything is possible.

Now grab those pom-poms, and all together now...

Go! (clap) Fight! (clap) Win! (clap, clap, clap)
GO! (clap) FIGHT! (clap) WIN! (clap, clap, clap)

You've got this coach! Be the CheerLEADER your team needs, wants, and deserves.

AFTERWORD

I recently was asked to speak about leadership to a Women in Business group at my local university. For ninety minutes, I stood at the front of a lecture hall and energetically shared data, stories, and vulnerable tidbits about my professional career journey—and yes, of course, I brought my pom-poms (although in this instance, they stayed in my book bag). As a training facilitator and keynote speaker, I feed off my audience; I alter my delivery based on nonverbal and verbal cues I receive. According to the fifty-plus faces staring blankly at me, this session was not going well. My message didn't seem to be resonating, and that crushed me inside. It didn't feel that long since I had been a senior in college, envisioning what the rest of my life would look like and preparing to transition into a new world of work. I was so excited to share that journey—including my mistakes and triumphs—with this group of bright, young women.

I opened up about everything: how I worked to build confidence in my leadership competencies, my erratic path to becoming an entrepreneur and author, learnings from the world of education and HR, the fact that I am a domestic abuse survivor and how that continues to shape my worldview still twenty years later, and how serving as chair of a school board during COVID taught me important leadership lessons about empathy—and how it almost broke me. Most importantly, I encouraged them to fail spectacularly because those are the moments that help you grow.

Crickets.

Or so I thought.

As we neared the end of our time together, I opened the floor to discussion, and signs of life began to emerge. Hands raised, and each woman shared a thoughtful question or story. I could see them connecting their experiences to mine, and that was just the beginning.

That evening, and over the next couple of days, my email and LinkedIn inboxes were blowing up with messages from many who attended:

"I feel so inspired."

"I learned so much."

"It really resonated with me and I appreciate you!"

"I plan to use your suggestions in my everyday life and future career."

"I felt lit up with a renewed fire!"

I was blown away. After every training session, I provide feedback forms, and the majority of the time participants are quite positive about the experience, but these messages had a different vibe and feel.

Ninety minutes had made a major impact. It was overwhelming and humbling.

One message that hit me especially hard was, "On the walk home from your presentation I didn't even listen to music, just walked in silence thinking about the changes I was going to make that you inspired!"

Wow. Obviously, no matter what I felt during our time spent together, the impact had been profound for those in the room. And then I realized why. My presentation had followed the CheerLEADERship model.

I connected with these young women, sharing honest stories relevant to their own experiences. I demonstrated care, opening up about mistakes I had made in an effort to help them avoid them. I challenged them to take risks and get out of their comfort zones in order to grow. I celebrated and highlighted wins they had thus far in their college careers, and let them know plenty more would come. But most importantly, I inspired them. I gave them someone to look up to, flaws and all; I told them the professional road would be bumpy, but with persistence, flexibility, and confidence, they could and would succeed. They knew I wasn't feeding them BS. I believed in them, which in turn created space for them to believe in themselves during the critical juncture of transitioning from college to work.

That evening, I was their CheerLEADER.

The road to publishing *CheerLEADERship: Strategies to*

Build and Support Human-Centric Workplaces for the Future has been a long one, but I can't tell you how much it means to me that you chose to read it and have come this far. I hope you have discovered your inner CheerLEADER, and with insights and activities shared, feel you are now prepared to guide and lead in a different way that makes work better.

I said it in the beginning, and I'll say it again: Leadership isn't "one size fits all," but it is my hope that you have found value in my stories and insights and will find ways to weave CheerLEADERship strategies into your everyday leadership practices. I encourage you to keep our humanness at the center, embrace a growth mindset, continue asking yourself and your teams reflective questions to deepen understanding, trust, and connection, and choose to be a lifelong learner on your leadership journey.

I'll be cheering for you!

APPENDIX

📣 COMPLETE THE SENTENCE

1. I love when we have the opportunity to collaborate with...because...

   _____
   _____
   _____
   _____
   _____
   _____

2. My favorite thing about working for my company is...

   _____
   _____
   _____
   _____
   _____
   _____

3. The qualities that best describe our team are...

   _____
   _____
   _____
   _____
   _____

4. Our team is most productive when...

   _____
   _____
   _____
   _____
   _____

5. Something I look forward to at work every week is...

   _____
   _____
   _____
   _____
   _____

6. When things get heavy, I can count on my team members to...

   _____
   _____
   _____
   _____
   _____

7. Since I started with my company, I have learned the following about myself...

_____
_____
_____
_____

8. The project I am most excited about tackling this year is...because...

_____
_____
_____
_____

9. One thing our team does really well is...

_____
_____
_____
_____

10. Our team gets a big laugh out of...

_____
_____
_____
_____

📣 IDEAS FOR ONBOARDING SUCCESS

PRE-ONBOARDING

- Stay connected to new hires throughout preboarding via email, texts, and a check-in phone call.
- Send company swag to the new hire's home a week or two ahead of their start day.
- Email the new hire a personalized welcome video from a member of the C-suite leadership.
- Email important first-day details including:
  - Dress code.
  - Parking information.
  - Check-in procedures.
  - Orientation agenda.
- Provide an organizational chart with names and contact information.

ONBOARDING: DAY ONE

- Decorate the member's desk/cubicle/office with fun and bright "welcome" signs.
- Have business cards and a name placard waiting in the designated work area.
- Book an early appointment with IT to ensure technology and log-in information are functional.
- Schedule a time for a casual meet and greet with team members.
- Have the new hire fill out a "work preferences" sheet, including:
  - Most productive time of day?

- Special dates to be aware of? (Birthday, anniversary, holidays, etc.).
- How do you like to be celebrated? (Coffee, cake, gift cards, etc.).
- Work pet peeves?
- What motivates you?
- How do you like to receive feedback?
- What do you hope to learn about this role/this company by the end of your first week?
- What questions do you have?
- Review "work preferences" one-on-one at the end of the first day.

ONBOARDING: WEEK ONE

- Preload meetings on the new hire's calendar with departmental leaders.
- Provide a checklist of 30/60/90-day actions and activities to help educate and engage the new hire in company culture.
- Assign the new hire a peer mentor.
- Have an end-of-week one-on-one with the new hire to check in on progress, learnings, and questions.

📣 WHAT COULD GO WRONG?

ACTION	WHAT COULD GO WRONG?	IMPACT

ABOUT THE AUTHOR

Stefanie Adams is a leadership development coach, facilitator, keynote speaker, former elected official, adjunct university instructor, entrepreneur, wife, and mother. For those who know her best, she is "Cheerleader Stef," which personifies her personality and leadership style. She has over twenty years of experience leading and training in corporate, nonprofit, and government settings. Due to her passion for DEI, she earned an M.Ed. in Multicultural Education in 2008, and her professional affiliations include the Society for Human Resource Management (SHRM). She is also a certified Forté Communication Coach.

In early 2020, Stefanie launched WNY People Development. In her role as Chief Empowerment Officer, she provides leadership training, coaching, and keynote presentations to grow the next generation of leaders. Her main areas of expertise are first-time/frontline manager development, women in leadership, engaging multigenerational workforces, and building high-impact teams.

She has worked as an organizational consultant for Johns Hopkins University School of Education in Baltimore, Maryland, and as Director of Customized Training for Cape Fear Community College in Wilmington, North Carolina. Most recently, she led the corporate training function for CastleBranch, also in Wilmington.

Stefanie is highly involved in her southeastern North Carolina community. She has served on multiple nonprofit boards centering around youth services, and, in 2022, she was nominated for a YWCA Women of Achievement Award in recognition of her work as school board chair during the COVID pandemic. As part of her community outreach, she also offers free leadership development for nonprofits in and around Wilmington.

Stefanie's days are fueled by coffee, yoga, new challenges, and building relationships. Her passions are developing others, serving the community, Philly sports, travel, managing the chaos that comes with life, kitchen dancing, and bringing positive energy into every room.